SONSHIP
THE STRATEGY OF SUBMISSION

Johnasen L. Pack

Unless otherwise noted, all Scriptures are from the Holy Bible, New Living Translation, copyright © 1996. Used by permission of Tyndale House Publishing, Inc. Wheaton, Illinois 60189. All rights reserved.

Scriptures noted KJV is taken from the KING JAMES VERSION of the Bible. Scriptures noted NIV are taken from the NEW INTERNATIONAL VERSION of the Bible.

Published by:
MAC PUBLISHING
www.macpub.org

SONSHIP, THE STRATEGY OF SUBMISSION
ISBN-10: 0985027789
ISBN-13: 978-0-9850277-8-0

TABLE OF CONTENTS

FORWARD

"Pastor Johnasen L. Pack is one of the clarion prophetic and apostolic voices of our day. Gifted with keen scriptural insight, his approach to issues of sonship, submission, servitude and covenant relationships reflects the heart of God and gives clear and accurate revelation of the person of Jesus Christ! Born out of personal sacrifice, rejection and betrayal, Johnasen is a rare commodity in the Kingdom of God: a father who knows how to be a son and a masterful technician in the Word who knows how to be a servant with true integrity, humility and honor. Because he thinks it not robbery to be called a son, we are the beneficiaries of the rich and fervent anointing upon his life."

Apostle Sherman C. Allen
Christ Cathedral Church
Fort Worth, Texas

ACKNOWLEDGEMENTS

I want to thank God: I never wanted to be a preacher, pastor, or author. I am simply amazed by how you refuse our NO, and sovereignly get your will accomplished. Thank you for every gift, talent, victory, and scar. I am blown away by your love for me and will always seek to please you by giving unto others, what you have given unto me. I will never lose my praise!

To my parents: Thank you all for the inherited gifts, charisma, and abilities that you have transferred to me. I am humbled because you all took hits and made sacrifices so I wouldn't have to. I am currently in Texas as a result of the path that was paved by my father. Thank you Dad, for teaching me to "Not let my past, Mess up my future." Mom, you are my #1 supporter and your gift of love and acts of generosity has served as a guide for me and made thousands the better. I love you!!

To my spiritual parents: Apostle and Co-Pastor Allen
I want to appreciate you all for your love and support publicly and privately. I was not able to write this without you being in my life. I have been challenged greatly to be better because of your impartations, standard, and example. I pray that I make you proud!

My family, My children: After all is said and done. The cameras are off, the members have left, and the building is locked, you are there. I appreciate how much you give back to me after I have given to so many. When this task became seemingly overwhelming for me, leaving an inheritance for you became my motivation. Know that I am proud of you and know that every sacrifice I make is with you in mind!

Spiritual Children, BBIC: I know I am not the easiest person to deal with at times, but my sincere desire is for you to be far greater than I. I see so much of me in you all and I am totally committed to doing all I can to help you become who you've been destined to become before the foundations of the world. Your love and support has helped to heal me, encourage me, and push me and I am grateful for it. As you read this book, know that you helped write with me. Remember... Something Good Has Already Happened!

Special Thanks: Pastor Bennie Moore, Bishop Yardley Griffin, Bishop David Martin, Bishop Anthony Willis, Prophet Terrell Turner, Bishop Henry Porter, Apostle Sammy Smith, Bishop Randy Borders, Bishop Kenneth Yelverton, Bishop Kenneth Spears, Overseer Elvis Bowman, Pastor Robert Jointer, Apostle Joshua Stewart, Bishop Garry Tyson, Dr. Kenneth Reid, and countless others who have helped me to birth the assignment of **"SONSHIP"** and the authority our authorship.

INTRODUCTION

One of the most profound revelations that I have discovered in scripture is the revelation of Sonship. Locked into this simple expression of relationship hold strategies to help establish order, sustain success, and leave legacy. As a student of the Bible, you must learn that what is important to God, must be important to you. As it is a proven fact that Sonship is important to God. When God decided to start a world, He planted a son in the garden. When God wanted to fix the world, He sent His only begotten son that whosoever believeth in him should not perish but have everlasting life.

Sonship is the strategy in which God has decided to transfer an inheritance from one person or entity to the next. The danger in this is, we have misused and abused this area of submission for personal and unproductive gain. Is act of abuse was never in the plan of God. Although Sonship has been abused by some, it's right and must be valued by the parent and the pupil.

Through personal experiences and biblical studies, I have learned to value the strategy of submission and attribute it as the secret to my success. All of my experiences have not been good, but they have all worked together for my good and after reading this book, I know it will do the same for you. As a servant leader, I have discovered that being in authority and under authority is genius.

Your intrest in reading this book is a complement in and of itself. My heart's desire is that you would be open to the truths that will be revealed, apply the principles immediately, and then wait for the intended results. You will discover that you have already been operating in certain areas already, and will see other areas you need to improve in. This will increase your visibility and value in the place in which you serve.

Your leader will take notice in your differences and be made the better because of it. My prayer is that you will not apply these principle just to be seen, but will allow these principles to become a part of your daily efforts. You will hopefully get a good word from the person you consider as a Pastor, but you will get an inheritance from the one you call father. If you are going to be in the relationship, you might as well get the most out of it. Let the journey begin!

1

THE ABC'S OF SONSHIP

In this chapter I want to deal with the ABC's of sonship. I will deal with the basics of what people should understand as it relates to sonship. A son is defined as an inherited one. The term is not gender specific but it speaks to a certain position. The working definition that we are going to use for this book is: Sonship - one that practices and heeds to a volunteered relationship of submission in order to qualify for an inheritance.

Here are the ABC's of sonship that we are going to look at:

- Answering the call of God to sonship. This is something that God ordains and not something that man makes. We have to understand that it is a calling and we have to value that particular calling.

- Believing in the father that God has placed you to be the son to. God will establish the relationships and place you under someone. He will place you under someone that is not perfect and who has flaws. God will put you under someone because He understands your expected end. One of the things you have to understand is that as a son you are not able to be your own watchman of your soul. You may understand your purpose in life, your goals, desires, fears, reluctances, or even your prejudices but God knows who to put you under that will be a help to you.

- Conduct yourself as a son. You have to make sure that you are properly submitting, honoring, and functioning in order to get the benefits of sonship.

Let's look at John 1:12-13(NKJV): *"But as many as received Him, to them He gave the right to become children of God, to those who believe in His name: who were born, not of blood, nor of the will of the flesh, nor of the will of man, but God."*

There are some things in these two scriptures that I will point out. First, you will never receive properly from someone that you perceive incorrectly. Whenever God places a person in your life you will have to make sure that you perceive them properly. You can not perceive them out of your flesh or your momentary feelings. You have to know who God has placed them in your life to be. When you are able to perceive them as a gift from God and a divine connection then you will know what God is counting on you to be a steward over. When God sends you a father he wants you to be a steward over that particular relationship.

Everyone in this passage of scripture did not value Jesus' uniqueness but those that did were given the right to become sons. While Jesus was opening up blinded eyes, unstopping deaf ears, and becoming a famous miracle worker there were still many that didn't believe in Him. They didn't believe because He came from the wrong place, He didn't look like everyone else, or function like everyone else. The Bible says *"But as many as received Him"* because again you cannot receive properly from who you perceive incorrectly. So, when they perceived Him properly the Bible says that He gave them power to become the sons of God.

One of the things that I want to tell you is, do not try to submit to someone because of who they are to someone else. Sonship is a personal calling. Speaking from my own personal experiences, I could not submit to someone just because they had blessed, were there for, or provided security for someone else. I had to make sure that I knew who they were to me and what God was calling them to be to me. When I was youthful and immature I found myself going with the masses. I never will forget that there was a man of God that I saw doing great things in the kingdom and I began to ask people who he was, and what is he like. Everyone began telling me that he was a great man of God and he will be there if you need him and all that good stuff. However, when I started trying to figure out if that was a genuine connection for me and reaching out I never got that same perception back.

So, you want to make sure that when you are picking someone or coming into covenant with someone that you do not choose based upon what had been done for someone else. You have the make sure that God has set that person in your life to make sure that they provide you with what God's will is concerning you. Again do not try to submit to someone because of who they are to someone else.

Joining someone who is becoming takes a whole lot of guts. When you look at the ministry of Jesus in this passage He was becoming great. He was not famous yet as far as His place in the religious fraternity or Christianity. Yes, He was opening up blinded eyes and unstopping deaf ears but to the masses and the religious sect He was not that valuable. So, when you find a leader that is becoming and God tells you to submit to them it takes a whole lot of guts. It is easy to submit to someone that is pastoring 10,000 people, is on the major networks of television and radio, and has 20,000 followers on twitter.

It is very easy to follow someone who has already become, but God may be entrusting you to partner with someone that is on their way. They may not have a large church but they have a heart for you. They may not be a multimillionaire but they have a heart for you. So, you have to make sure that when God is showing you someone that is becoming that you do not become carnal and sensual in your view. If you do then you will miss the right perception because you are looking at the kind of car that they drive, the house that they live in, the amount of members that they have, or where they are preaching. You have to make sure that you are able to properly perceive them as the person that God put in your life.

So, again it is easy to follow someone that is proven or popular but can you follow someone because that is the right fit for you. What I have discovered is that God will never partner you with someone when there is no mutual exchange. If God is causing them to become, then you are a part of the help needed to assist them to get wherever it is that they need to go. That is why joining someone who is becoming takes a whole lot of guts.

The privilege of being a son is uncomfortably comfortable. I cannot say that as a submitted son that I am always comfortable. I don't always like being rebuked. Sometimes there are some things that I want to do on my own. I preach all across the country and I travel but I still make sure that I am submitted. I never make any major decisions as it relates to my personal life or even my ministry without bouncing it off of my man of God. I believe that my gift to see is for everyone else but history has shown that I have not done the best job at seeing for me. It is because my gift works on so many other people that I have to trust that the same way that those that are submitted to me come to me for fatherly counsel that I go to him. That is because I am not just in authority, I am under authority and at times it is uncomfortable because I don't always agree. I don't always understand. Sometime when I don't understand I am not always given an explanation. Sometimes I have to just trust that his viewpoint and his word for my life are right.

I understand that I cannot receive the blessing prophecies that he gives to me and not receive his rebukes. It is uncomfortably comfortable but it is a God thing. It is not something that I would have done on my own. When I was connected to my spiritual father it was during a time when I wasn't looking for a father. I had just been hurt and had just gone through some major transitions. I had to tough it out and do a lot on my own as I had done my entire life. So, when God sent him into my life I wasn't looking for a father and honestly he wasn't looking for a son. Yet it was my responsibility to make sure because I knew that God was turning something in my spirit. I had to answer that particular call and then submit myself to the man of God.

I want you to understand that when God puts a spiritual father or mother into your life they don't have to be older, the same ethnicity, or even have the same style or gifting as you. They just have to have a heart for you and an desire to do all that they can to help you to be better than them.

One of the things that I love about the story about John the Baptist and Jesus was how it revealed the power of connection. We understand that Jesus is the son of God, Emmanuel which is God with us. Jesus was illegitimate as it relates to doing public ministry in the earth because He was from the wrong tribe. In that day you had to be from the tribe of Levi or the Levitical tribe but Jesus was from the tribe of Judah. So, He had to submit Himself to someone from the tribe of Levi so that He could gain authorization in the earth to do ministry.

What He did was He went out to find John the Baptist. When He found John the Baptist He went to him so that He could submit to him. Now, I need you to understand that John the Baptist didn't have a large church but he had a ministry. As a matter of fact he didn't have a church at all but he was doing ministry in the wilderness. John didn't wear the finest clothes. He just wore the most recent animal that he had killed. He didn't get manicures or pedicures. He didn't eat at the finest restaurants but he ate locusts and wild honey. However, even though John didn't have the look he was legit. (That is a word for somebody!) When God places someone in your life you will have to perceive them beyond the look. Just because they have the look does not mean that they have legitimacy.

Jesus partnered Himself with John the Baptist. He went to him and said you have to baptize Me so that the scripture can be fulfilled. John said I don't want to baptize you because I understand who you are and I am not even worthy to tie your shoes. However, Jesus said that in order for the scripture to be fulfilled we have to go through this particular act of protocol. Now, I need you to understand that John the Baptist baptized people but he never did miracles. Jesus worked miracles but He never baptized. To understand their relationship you have to realize that John the Baptist is the baptizing one and Jesus is the miracle worker but when they partnered together there was an explosion in the Jordan. The Bible says that God said that this is My beloved Son in whom I am well pleased. Understand that even though they were different when they joined together they were able to do something that caused the heavens to open.

So, you as a prophet trying to find another prophet or trying to find someone that flows like you flow have to understand, that does not always suggest, that is a God connection for you. Again, John and Jesus is a primary example that if it is a God connection, and if both people play their role, and submit to the order of God, then there will be an explosion and the heavens are going to open. Again, they don't have to be older than you, the same ethnicity as you, or even have the same style or gifting as you.

I have learned from a very successful pastor in Dallas, Texas that one of the ways that you will know who your father or mother is will be because they will speak deeper into your spirit than anyone else. It is not about who is the greatest voice as far as crowds. I know some of the greatest preachers in the country and as a second generation preacher and a student of preaching I listen to some of everyone. I listen to different styles, denominations, and even other religions. However, what I have discovered is that when my man of God gets up to preach he speaks deeper into my spirit than anyone else.

CONVERSATION STARTERS

In your own words, define what SONSHIP means to you.

_____
_____
_____
_____

What does the A stand for?

_____
_____
_____
_____

What does the B stand for?

_____
_____
_____
_____

What does the C stand for?

_____
_____
_____
_____

How do you know that you and your leader are supposed to be connected?

_____
_____
_____
_____

How would you define SUBMISSION in your own words?

_____

_____

_____

_____

Explain the relationship you had with your natural father.

_____

_____

_____

_____

Has this affected your SONSHIP in any way? If so, list how.

_____

_____

_____

_____

Explain the effects from a previous spiritual father, if any.

_____

_____

_____

_____

What was the hardest lesson you had to learn regarding SONSHIP?

_____

_____

_____

_____

Do you believe that you need to understand or agree with your leader to obey their instructions?

_____

_____

_____

_____

How do you believe your connection has helped or will you?

_____

_____

_____

_____

How do you believe your connection has helped or will help your leader?

_____

_____

_____

_____

2

WHEN YOUR LEADER IS IN TRANSITION

I want to talk about when your leader is in transition. Let's look at the scriptural base for this which is 2 Samuel 21:15-17(NKJV):

"When the Philistines were at war again with Israel, David and his servants with him went down and fought against the Philistines; and David grew faint. Then Ishbi-Benob, who was one of the sons of the giant, the weight of whose bronze spear was three hundred shekels, who was bearing a new sword, thought he could kill David. But Abishai the son of Zeruiah came to his aid, and struck the Philistine and killed him. Then the men of David swore to him, saying, You shall go out no more with us to battle, lest you quench the lamp of Israel."

This is one of the messages that I have been preaching across the country. I believe that in most cases when leaders are in transition that it takes the people that are connected to them to know how to handle their particular transition. In this chapter I am going to explain how to move when your leader moves because some of the moves they make will not always be verbal. Some of the moves, you are just going to have to catch based upon your knowledge of who they are, what God is sharing with you, and your ability to discern the moment.

I believe what we have to understand is that leaders are always evolving. They never stay the same. As they continue to walk with God they will continue to transition. We have to know that if we transition as sons then our fathers will transition as well. One of the statements that hindered the growth of my pastoral ministry in certain seasons was people saying I know my dad. Those people were basically saying who my dad was, is who my dad will always be. Just because I was a thing or liked doing things a certain way does not mean that is the way that I always wanted things to be or the way I would always be.

When people say that they know their leader real well what they are honestly saying is I have a good understanding of who they were or who they are at that moment. However, they need to stay open and understand that God may cause their leader to change. God may change their desires, taste, or their protocol if you will because they have evolved into another form of who they are. So, when leaders are transitioned you have to know that even though you may have known them you may not always know them. (Let me say that again!) Just because you have known them, you've walked with them, you've been in their ministry for years, you are a part of their family, and you've shared in private moments does not mean that you will always know your leaders.

So, their motives were pure but my sons did not recognize that I was always evolving. They didn't mean any harm but they had to realize that I was always evolving even from the way I dressed to my private prep time. There were times when I first started ministry that I dressed very loud and very creative. Then when I started moving into pastoral ministry and business my dressing got more conservative. My prep time changed from where I use to talk a lot before I ministered but then I went through seasons were they wondered why I didn't talk as much. It was because I was evolving and doing things differently so they had to pay attention to my moods and my movements to be able to evolve with me.

Even my personal preferences changed as far as how I handle business and meetings. There were times when my health was challenged and I could not meet with everyone before and after I ministered. As I transitioned I was more open as a pastor to meet and share with other people but my sons had to evolve with me. So, if I can encourage a son that is connected to a father I want to tell you to pay close attention to the details. Again, know that just because you have known them doesn't mean that you will always know them.

Those sons that are able to evolve with their fathers must remain close to them. You have to keep the lines of communication open. You have to call just see if they are ok. You have to ask what they need and how they want things done. You can not become so mechanical that you lock yourself into doing things one way and thinking that it is going to be that way all the time. So, again those that are able to evolve must remain close to your leader.

Some people do not have the testimony of being close because leaders like being around people who can discern and not those that always have to be told what to do. When people are able to discern the moment then as a leader you will know that they are praying for you, paying close attention to you, and that their purpose is to be connected to you. Those are the people that the leaders will pull close. If they are not able to be pulled close that means that they need constant explanation, constant affirmation, and constant conformation.

When a leader is transitioning they don't always have time to explain because as God is transitioning them He is not telling them everything in completion. The leader has to take steps in evolution and just try things. That is why the leader needs people that are connected to him to be able to discern so that again they are evolving as he is evolving. Once the sons recognize that the leader is transitioning if the leader can explain it then he will but if he cannot then the sons are still responsible to transition with them. Leaders are always preparing for the next battle, test, effort, and opportunity.

While the children of Israel were getting ready to fight again David's mind was on the next battle. Like David you will appreciate where you are but then something will always be telling you that there is something that is coming next or is going to happen next. We have to make sure that as we are progressing in life and accomplishing things that we take moments to celebrate our successes. That way when it is time to prepare for the next battle the joy of the journey will not be overlooked. You have to experience the joy of the journey in order to be able to move on. Remember that leaders are always preparing for the next battle.

In 2 Samuel Israel was under attack by the Philistines again but this time David was tired. David was known as the warrior and a person that gave his life for what he believed in. As a boy David was tending his father's sheep and killed a lion and a bear because the lion and the bear came after the sheep that he was called to be a steward over. (Let me say that again!) It was not his sheep that he was tending but his father's sheep. When the lion and the bear came to kill those sheep because David was the steward over the sheep he killed the lion and the bear on his father's behalf. As the leader transitions and entrust you with moments of service you will have to understand that you will have to fight and kill things as if they were your own. Whenever the lion and the bear came David didn't go in the house to get his father Jesse and tell him that they were under attack. He took it upon himself to fight the lion and the bear because he had been entrusted with that particular assignment.

Then the Bible says that David goes to serve his brothers and finds out that Goliath is taunting the children of Israel. David asked the question, "What will the man get that kills the giant?" Once he hears what the reward will be he decides to go fight Goliath. He goes to Saul and tells him that he will fight the giant. Saul tries to put his armor on David and the armor doesn't fit. So David goes into battle with a sling shot and five smooth stones. The Bible says that David hits Goliath in the head with one of the stones then cut his head off to take it back to Saul. The Bible then goes on to say that David has killed his ten thousands while Saul has killed his thousands.

David was always fighting and was known as a warrior. However, in 2 Samuel 21:15-17 this time as David was going into battle he was tired. I want to make sure that we understand this word tired. You have to know the difference between when your leader is tired because of fatigue and when your leader is tired because of transition. (Let me say that again!) You will have to discern when your leader is tired because of fatigue (not getting enough rest, they are stressed, or going though something) or if they are tired because of the realm that they have functioned in before is a realm that they have to graduate from.

When a leader is use to doing certain things or just handling all matters, when they start to evolve into another place normally they will first get tired, irritated, and moody. They may not always understand why but it is because they are pregnant with something greater. In the natural realm when a woman is pregnant she will began to get uncomfortable. She will no longer be able to fit into what she use to fit into. She will not be able to walk as much as she is used to. She's uncomfortable because her body is now out growing what she use to be so that she can birth out something that is coming. So, you have to discern that your leader's irritation may not always be a product of them just being tired, in need of rest, or in need of a vacation. It might be that they just need somebody that is submitted to them to step up and do what they should no longer be doing.

Your leader might be trying to graduate and you are keeping them in the twelfth grade because you will not take it upon yourself to grab that particular area in ministry, assignments, or responsibilities from your leader. You just want to sit back and celebrate that the leader handles everything so well. I strongly believe that even though David was tired had he went out to fight Ishbi-Benob again that he would have won the battle because that was just the kind of warrior that he was. However, just because he would have won doesn't mean that he was supposed to fight. (Let me say that again!) Just because David would have won the battle doesn't mean that he was supposed to fight.

The tiredness was an indication that he was in a place that he needed to graduate from. David had been a shepherd, a servant, and a warrior but now he was a king. It took someone that was submitted to him to understand his transition and do something about it. David didn't make an announcement to the children of Israel to tell them that God had transitioned him. He didn't tell them hey I am in another place in my life and I need you to step up and help me do something different. David just prepared to go to battle like he did in times past. I have discovered that this kind of tiredness that he had is sometimes downplayed as just fatigue. That's when we will just tell the leader that you have to get some rest and you know you have to take care of yourself.

We have to understand this truth that when we evolve we have to evolve into who we are supposed to be. That means that we may not always be able to be the person that we use to be or do the things we use to do because we have to know how to evolve. I have heard several times well if you would have told me to do it then I would have done it. I believe this statement was said only to win some kind of brownie points. The leader is not always able to say I need help because they are so use to taking on the burden of the ministry and the assignment. They are used to making sure that everything is done. Leaders always say if it needs to be done then I am going to do it myself. However, if we as leaders always take that attitude then we don't give any room for evolution. That is how we die off because we are carrying too much of the old and are unable to open up our hands and carry to new.

Again, when the lion and the bear came to attack the sheep no one asked David to protect the sheep he just stepped up, took responsibility fought and won. He didn't ask anyone if he should fight the lion or the bear. He just took it upon himself to make sure that he protected what he had been put in charge over. When Goliath came against the children of Israel again he didn't ask anyone if he should fight. David just stepped up took responsibility fought and won.

Now, in 2 Samuel 21:15-17 the enemy was specifically after David. The lion and the bear were after all the sheep and Goliath was after all of the children of Israel or the church. However, now Ishbi-Benob was specifically after David. The question is if David had always fought for the church would the church now protect David? What happens in most cases is the church expects the leader to stay in constant warfare to protect the people and themselves. (Let me say that again!) Leaders are having to protect the people and protect themselves because the enemy is specifically after them.

So, even though David was tired he would have went out and fought anyway. Again I believe that he would have won. However, the issue was not would he have won but was he supposed to be fighting. Leaders have routines and are familiar with fighting through distractions, disasters, and discouragement. The fight is not new to them but time reveals that the response to the fighting must be new. Again, leaders function in routines. They are familiar with fighting through distractions, opinions, and accusations. They are use to dealing with disasters, having problems in their lives and families yet still having to preach. They deal with discouragement and sometimes not feeling good enough. They deal with rejection when they are not received properly. Leaders deal with all of this things yet they still get up and fight. However, what leaders now have to understand is that they have to evolve into another place in God and the people that are connected to them have to evolve as well.

CONVERSATION STARTERS

Define Transition.

_____
_____
_____
_____

What traits does your leader display when they are in transition?

_____
_____
_____
_____

How many major transitions have your leader went through since you've been connected?

_____
_____
_____
_____

Do you see yourself as important in the life of your leader? If so or if not, list why.

_____
_____
_____
_____

How important is your leader to you spiritually? Rate from 1-10.

_____
_____
_____
_____

How important is your leader to you naturally? Rate from 1-10.

_____
_____
_____
_____

How well do the people around you value your leader?

_____
_____
_____
_____

3

WHEN YOUR LEADER IS IN TRANSITION PART II

In today's society people are not carrying around swords but if you remove the "s" from the word swords you will be left with the word "words". Now instead of people coming after David with swords they are coming after the leader with words. People are saying dangerous things about their leaders. I know that it has been said that sticks and stones may break my bones, but words will never hurt me; well, that is a lie. Words do hurt; but the leader cannot afford to fight every battle that is coming against them. Someone that is connected to them has to be able to stand up and fight on their behalf.

Abishai stood up and he told David look you can no longer go out with us. I have to fight on your behalf because you are too valuable to me. If something were to happen to you then the light of Israel will be quenched. Now, what you have to understand about Abishai is that he was really David's nephew. However, as it relates to his responsibility of warfare and in this particular text, Abishai was not just functioning as a nephew. I believe that he was functioning as a son submitted to this particular move.

Abishai didn't have a lot of history in fighting, meaning that he is not famous, if you will. However, Abishai is connected to David because he was able to perceive how valuable David was to him. That is why he stepped up and he said something. He told David that you can no longer go out to battle with us, lest you quench the light of Israel. Abishai was not one of the main leaders but he was David's nephew and he reverenced who David was, so he spoke up.

One of the amazing things about this act was that when Abishai spoke up, no one else in the camp said anything. This is important because everything that the Lord places on your heart to do for your leaders will not always be received by the others. When God says this is what you need to do and you stand up and say this is how we need to make the adjustment, everybody may not comply. However, just because they don't comply or agree with you doesn't mean that you didn't hear from God properly or that you didn't have the particular remedy for that particular moment. That is why when Abishai spoke up and no one said anything is amazing.

God may use you as the one to shift that ministry, business, or group and because He is using you to shift it the majority may not always respond. This is important again because everything that the Lord places on your heart you cannot always expect to get people to cosign and believe in what you believe because they do not perceive the way you perceive. I believe that no one said anything because they were so familiar with David. They were preparing to go out to war with David but did not take into consideration that if anything would have happened to David then they would have been lost themselves.

Thank God the He raised up an Abishai to fight on David's behalf. Who David was to Abishai was clearly not who he was to the rest of them. (Let me say that again!) Clearly who David was to Abishai was clearly not who David was to everyone else. David was just a warrior to everyone else but to Abishai David was a valuable part of his life and to his journey. Abishai felt that he could not afford for David to be lost because of a battle that David was not suppose to be fighting.

David must have trusted Abiahai's motives and abilities or else he would have rejected his offer and fought anyway. This is important because even though you have a heart for your leader if you have not been proven to be trust worthy, been accountable, or faithful, they will not allow you the freedom to do things the way you see fit. If you are going to be in authority you have to first be under authority. So, David had to trust Abiahai's motives and abilities to say ok you go ahead and fight and I will stay back.

This is also important because my generation of preachers have become more focused on being talented whether then being trusted. However, trust will outweigh talent any day of the week. We have to make sure that as we are submitted that we are not just being talented. We have to make sure that we are not people that are just seeking the next mic, engagement, or the next opportunity but that we are seeking to be trusted. We never know when we are going to be the shift agent for the next transition.

The major questions that I want to ask are, what are you doing? What are you doing or what have you done to prove to your leader that you can be trusted? Do you follow instruction? Do you do things exactly the way that they said it or do you always add your own twist to it because you cannot properly follow? Do you pray for the leaders and their counsel when you are asked to bless an offering? Are you a person that always goes above and beyond what you are asked to do? Are you a person that can understand your moment and prove that you can be trusted in that moment? Are you on time for services, meetings, and appointments? If you are going to be absent do you let your leader know ahead of time that you will be absent? If you need to be excused do you get permission to be excused or do you just walk away and leave? Do you offer help when you are not asked to do something or do you only offer help when others are watching? Is your lifestyle opposite to the teachings and beliefs of your leader? Do you keep your word to your leader and to others? Have you developed a love for what he loves and who he loves? These are all questions that you must consider. You may have the remedy to the situation but you have to work to gain the respect of your leader. How do you handle getting rebuked? How do you handle when they don't agree with your ideas? Do you take your ball and go home or do you put a smile on your face and show others this is how you handle these particular moments for the betterment of the body?

Abishai had no previous history of fighting a giant but in his first fight he fought and won just like David did. I am thoroughly convinced that his victory was not so much about his ability but it was because of his motive. It was because in his heart his motives were to stand up on behalf of his leader and that caused him to fight and win. I strongly believe that you can not fight a battle in the name of your leader and lose. You will always win. (Let me say that again!) You will always win battles fought in the name of your leaders.

When Abishai won again, the people made a decision not to let David go out to battle again. You cannot wait for a committee to decide on when it is time for you to be a son. Abishai was not the commander of the army. So what if you are not the assistant pastor. So what if you are not the head trustee. Abishai was a son and as a son his job was to say I see my father in a particular light and I am not going to wait for someone to tell me who my father is to me. He perceive something about the moment. No one else may have noticed David's tiredness or that he was handling things different. It was only because Abishai did notice that he stepped up and did what needed to be done.

Again everyone will not see what you see because they don't perceive your leader the way you do. To some people your leader is just a preacher and to other they are just a pastor. However, to others they are real fathers and real mothers. So you have to take that into consideration. If you let the numbers hinder you then you are putting the life of your leader at risk. (Let me say that again!) If you say this is what I believe God is saying and when the multitudes doesn't agree if you let them tell you that you have not heard from God then you put your leader's life at risk.
One of the things that I have discovered about my spiritual father is although I love the people around him I have to love him through them. That is because my first responsibility is to love my leader and to make sure that the life of my leader is a long healthy

and prosperous life. It is because I understand that and I value my role that I can never allow my leader's life to be put at risk.

I have to say certain things even if it is going to make me look bad to others because my job is not to keep quiet because sometimes silence is affirmation. Silence can mean that you agree with what everyone else is saying. You have to stand up and sometimes risk being the odd ball because again your perception says who the leader is to you may not be what the leader is to everybody else. So, the next time the leader says that they are tired you have to discern whether this is the result of fatigue or whether this is the result of transition.

Because of your love for the person that God has connected you to He is going to speak to you at times. There will be times where God will speak something to you and you will have to go to your leader and say this is what God has showed me and told me. Your leader will look at you in amazement because while God was talking to them He was talking to you as well but you did not implement anything. This is important because Abishai still had to get permission even though he had the right word. So, just because you have an accurate word does not mean that you can immediately implement it.

He went to David and told him that I understand that you are in transition and so we need to do things another way and again Abishai was trusted. You have to make sure that when God gives you a word that you have access to your leaders and say this is what the Lord told me and this is the dream I had. I believe that this is something that the Lord is instructing us to do. Once you are able to communicate that then you have to trust that the one that you are submitted to will make the right decision in time. All things that are lawful are not always expedient so they might not immediately buy into what you have said. Or they may buy into what you have said but just tweak it based upon their discretion.

You have to make sure that if God has partnered you with a leader then as they evolve you have to evolve as well. This will be someone that is able to partner with and carry on in those areas that the leader has to graduate from. This is to make sure that there are no gaps in the transition and that all of you are flourishing and moving. You have to thank God for leaders that can transition. You have to thank God for people that just don't stay the same way and always do things the same way. You have to thank God for people that are able to be led by the Spirit.

The Bible says in Romans 8:14(NKJV): *"For as many as are led by the Spirit of God, these are the sons of God."*

Now the word Spirit there has a capital S which means the mind of God. So, when you are led by the mind of the person that you are submitted to that qualifies you to be a son. They may not say it out of their mouth but they will say it through their minds. The Bible also says that my sheep knows my voice. A sheep by nature is a dumb animal so the sheep needs the voice to constantly tell them how they should do it, when they should do it, how they should respond, and when they should respond. That is the way sheep functions.

Now, the sheep needs the voice but the son has to grab a hold to the mind of the leader. There are some things that will be on my leaders mind that I don't need them to say out of their mouth. I can see the look and the behavior because I am close and connected to them, I understand what that need or want. You want to make sure that you are able to be an important part in those transitions. If you can discern those moments then you will always evolve with them. If you miss those particular moments then you might not be a part of their evolution and you might miss moments to flourish. So I pray that you will understand that if God has connected you to them then as they transition then you will transition as well.

CONVERSATION STARTERS

Does your title define you?

_____

_____

_____

_____

How does your title or lack of a title help you in the area of SONSHIP?

_____

_____

_____

_____

How does your title or lack of a title help your leader in the area of SONSHIP?

_____

_____

_____

_____

What GIANT do you see as an obstacle in the season of you and your leader's life?

_____

_____

_____

_____

How do you plan on defeating this GIANT whether you receive help or not?

_____
_____
_____
_____

4

THE SUCCESSOR

In this chapter I want to deal with succession. One of the greatest pictures of succession is the story of Elijah and Elisha. In 1 Kings 19:19-21 and then 2 Kings 2:1-14 you will be able to find this particular story. I want to point out some things that are in these passages of scripture. One of the most significant things that I've found about the father and son connection is that sons don't just find fathers. What you have to understand about this connection is that a father must see something significant in the son. I think that we have to understand that we don't just walk around calling people dad that have not accepted us as sons.

The story of Elijah and Elisha is interesting because Elisha was minding his own business plowing with twelve yoke of oxen. The Bible tells us that Elijah knows that he is going to be in transition so he goes out to find a person that has the potential to be his successor and he finds Elisha. This is going to be the foundation of this particular teaching. The reason why most relationships don't last is because the sons goes out and finds their father based upon their preference. They look for someone that will do what they want them to do. Or they look for someone that presents what they want just at that particular time verses having a long term connection. That is why fathers must seek out sons and not just the son seeking a particular father.

When Elijah finds Elisha he finds him working because lazy people wanting an opportunity will never be chosen by someone of value. (Let me say that again!) Lazy people waiting on an opportunity will not be chosen by someone of value. Someone that is worth something will not invest worth into someone who is not worth it. They will have to see that the person that they want to sow into has something to bring to the table. Elijah finds Elisha working plowing with twelve yoke of oxen which reveals that he's capable of smoothly leading some of the most stubborn animals that exist. Oxen by nature are very difficult to deal with. They are big and very heavy to move. When Elijah saw Elisha working he had them smoothly moving in the direction that he desired for them to go in.

This may be a word for somebody because your ability to lead the stubborn successfully qualifies you for succession. (Let me say that again!) Because of your ability to lead stubborn individuals and problems qualifies you for succession. So if you quit because things are difficult you are showing your leader that you cannot handle pressure. When Elijah sees the work that Elisha was doing he throws his mantle on him then walks away and Elisha knew that something significant had taken place.

Elijah was like wow I see what he is doing and I see how he is accomplishing it. He is somebody that can handle the responsibility of the mantle that I am going to place on him. He throws the mantle on him and he walks away.

As a son you must value moments when your leader gives you an opportunity to be another part of them, see another part of them, or handle them in a certain way. You have to know how to recognize that moment. If a leader is normally private and they bring you into a private moment that is significant. If they never take you out to eat then they finally do, that is significant. If they are always professional and then one day they have a personal conversation with you that is significant. If you are always seeing them publically, but have never seen what goes on behind closed doors and then all of a sudden you are shown, you have to learn how to value that moment and also learn how to function in that moment.

So in the moment that Elijah sees Elisha and throws his mantle on him Elisha has to recognize that something significant has happened. Maybe your leader being transparent in their conversations or investments in you is more about exposing you to more of them and not just complimenting you for what you have been. You have to understand that they might be trying to reveal themselves and that moment is a moment where they are trying to see if you can catch it. This is not something that can be taken lightly because everything that your leader does or says is intentional. (Let me say that again!) Everything that your leader says or does is intentional. Every word, handshake, pat on the back, word of affirmation is intentional. It is loaded when they do it. So again I say that we cannot take this lightly.

So when Elijah throws the mantle on Elisha he does not follow Elisha but he walks away from him and expects Elisha to follow him. Now, this is important because fathers don't chase sons. They don't have time to call you and figure out why you are missing or not in place. A real father believes that you can make the most out of the moment and opportunity that they have afforded to you and then they will move. However, you have to make the most out of that moment and discern that something significant has just happened and that change now needs to take place.

Now, this is something that they could say or do to wake up something in you again to reveal that this is a transitional moment and change has to take place. Elisha wanted to go back. He knew that when the mantle was thrown on him that he was supposed to follow Elijah. However, he wanted to go back to kiss his father and mother and say goodbye. This is important as well. It speaks to the character and the volume of Elisha. Even though he knows that he is supposed to go with Elijah he desires to go back to make sure that he leaves the right way. It was because he had integrity that was proving something to Elijah. Elisha had to go back and handle things properly because you have to make sure that you leave the right way.

At my church, Bridge Builders International Church, I constantly teach them that in order to be a bridge builder you cannot be a bridge breaker. You have to make sure that you never burn a bridge because you never know who God is going to use in your future. That person may not provide a great level of significance now but you never know who you are going to need next. So, Elijah wanted to go back and say goodbye and when he went back he finished his assignment.

A real father will never tell you to dishonor your natural father. Your natural parents may not be the best. They may not even be saved, but a real father would never tell you to dishonor someone in that particular capacity. If they do then that is a clear indication that is not the father that God has placed over your life. (Let me say that again!) A real father will never tell you to dishonor your natural or former spiritual father. I have learned that if you are led or have been released to leave, do it right so that you can leave with the respect of the leader and of the people, if possible.

Elisha then followed Elijah to serve, to serve, to serve! Elijah put the mantle on Elisha and his job was to serve Elijah. This is important as it relates to succession because you cannot allow those that are connected to your leader to determine what kind of relationship you will have with that leader. Elisha's job was to serve and follow Elijah. Most novices miss the principle that you are promoted through service. This is why I tell people constantly that if you want to figure out what your real assignment is in God then don't get a mic, get a mop. Your job is to make sure that through service you prove that you can be trusted, that you are promotable, and that you are someone that is worth investing in. You have to know that you are promoted through service.

Most novices become celebrities and they work hard to be seen or to be next instead of working hard to be necessary. If you want to be next, the next name, or the next person that is flowing in leadership then you have to make sure that you are not working hard to just be next. You have to make sure that you are not just trying to position yourself with the "who's who" but that you are working hard to be necessary. You will end up growing behind the scenes when no one is paying attention to you. When you are on the back side of the desert or you have your moments where you don't feel sure of yourself, make sure that you are working hard to be necessary. Work hard to be someone significant that brings something to the table that will make a difference. You have to make sure that you understand this.

Elijah chose Elisha specifically but still took him through a process. When Elijah threw the mantle on Elisha he could have told Elijah, "ok I'm already ready so let's just go and do great things for God." However, it was not Elisha's time to be promoted as far as being Elijah's successor. He had to go through the process to be Elijah successor. I want to show you how he was processed. On four separate occasions Elijah tells Elisha, "I am going to a particular destination. I want you to stay here and I will be back to get you." Elisha says to him, "As long as your soul lives I'm not leaving you."

That is important because as I have said previously, you have to discern what your leader is saying. Even though Elijah told him to stay he needed Elisha to discern that it was a test. Elijah needed to know if he knew more about what he meant then what he was saying. This was not an act of disrespect because the father wanted the son to know what he meant and not just hearing what he was saying. There have been times where I have asked to leave a service early. I was told yes, that I could leave however, I heard no in my leader's voice. So I knew that I needed to be in place. I canceled my plans and showed up anyway. They had said yes to appease me because they knew that I really wanted to be somewhere else. Yet, I knew it was just a test to see if I knew what they meant instead of what they were saying.

So when I showed up at the service anyway after I was told that I could leave my leader looked at me like they were surprised that I was there. Then gave me a look like they were pleased and that look will be remembered for the rest of my life. My leader was teaching me that in transition I am to show myself able to be respected because I know what they mean by their looks and gestures. That there is a different thing being communicated other than what they were saying.

On these four occasions Elijah tells Elisha, "You stay here. I'm going to another place." The Bible says that he kept following Elijah and when Elijah saw this he said, "well I guess it's now time for me to succeed." The Bible says that people were even telling Elisha don't you know that Elijah is getting ready to leave you. They started trying to create doubt in the mind of Elisha. However, when you know your assignment to the leader you never listen to other people, you always listen and respond to what your leader is saying to you so you know what to do next.

The Bible says that Elijah is getting ready to be taken up in a whirlwind. As he is going up Elisha says to him my father, my father. Now, you have to know that even though he has followed Elijah through all of these transitions he had never called him father. This is important because he saw Elijah as the leader but then when Elijah got ready to transition he saw him as a father that was leaving. When Elisha sees Elijah properly he calls him what he is based upon his perception.

You have to properly perceive in order to properly receive. So as Elijah is taken up in the whirlwind the Bible says that Elisha says my father, my father because he is going to inherit his mantle. He was not going to just catch the mantle but he was going to inherit the mantle. A son is an inherited one so the mantle will not just come to a leader or a position holder or a member. The mantle will go to a son. So when he says my father, my father he qualifies himself to be a son so he got the mantle. He receives what was on the leader which was the leaders light, blessing, and spirit. All of this was embodied in Elisha because he served and because he was able to discern and not just go off of what was said but what was meant. The Bible says that once he caught the mantle he did something that I encourage all of you to do. When you get the mantle of the leader don't start over start where they left off.

Elisha then goes to the water and he smote the waters like he saw Elijah do it. He smote the waters and says where is the God of Elijah. Now, because he is new on the scene he didn't have as much clout as anyone else. When he had the mantle which represented the light of Elijah he was able to pick up where Elijah left off. We know that Elijah worked 16 miracles and then Elisha worked 32 miracles. That was because Elisha picked up where Elijah left off and he didn't just do what Elijah did. Elisha did double of what Elijah did because he followed in the footsteps of his father.

This is important because what you call them is based upon what you perceived them to be. I bless God because my pastor is not only my pastor, my bishop, my apostle, my prophet or my teacher but at the end of the day that's my dad. Based upon that I believe that my relationship as a son is greater then my relationship as a pastor. So based upon who I perceive them to be that is what I called them to be. I encourage you that if you are going to qualify for succession one of the main things you can do is know what is meant and not just what is said.

You have to hear when they say "I'm ok" that there is something else going on. You have to hear when they say "I am going through." You have to discern that moment because you have been walking with them. You have tuned out everybody else because the enemy will send people in your life to get you disconnected from your leader. They see that you are the next one.

They see that you are the successor. They see that you are the one that is going to take things to the next level. They do this because of their own insecurities or their own agendas. They will try to move you out of the way to position their own selves where you are meant to be. I am so glad that Elisha did not pay attention to the other prophets that were trying to disconnect him but he stayed true to Elijah. When Elijah ascends he calls him my father, my father, he accepts the mantle and picks up where Elijah left off.

If you are going to succeed you have to understand that you cannot be lazy. You have to be working where you are. That difficult moment that you are in might be the moment that is qualifying you for where God is getting ready to take you. With those oxen you have to learn that although it is difficult you don't let people run you away because you are being qualified and molded. Don't let them run you away from that ministry, that group, or that church. You take that difficult matter and you go back to learn how to perfect it because you don't know who's watching. You don't know when your moment of opportunity is going to come.

You have to make sure that if God tells you to leave anything that you leave the right way so that the blessing can still be in the transition. Then you have to discern. You have to discern what they are saying. Even through you hear it you have to know it. This takes time and it takes someone that has a heart to serve. The mantle of Elijah didn't just go from one prophet to the next. It went from a father to a son and that is how you succeed. If you apply these principles then succession is in your future. As they go up you are going to go up with them.

Now, there is one last thing that I want to say about succession. I use to think that the leader had to die off in order to leave the mantle. However, now I further understand that every time a leader elevates then they leave something for the person after them to transition with them. As a leader goes up you go up with them. So when you have a progressive person that is able to go from one place to another then your job if you are under them is to move into that next place. Those that are under you will move into that next place. Then we will have no gaps or errors but we will function in proper succession. Again, if you do this, succession is in your near future.

CONVERSATION STARTERS

Why was Elijah looking for a successor?

_____

_____

_____

_____

What was Elisha doing when Elijah found him?

_____

_____

_____

_____

Define the character of an ox.

_____

_____

_____

_____

Define what the word plowing means.

_____

_____

_____

_____

What is a mantle?

_____

_____

_____

_____

How well do you maximize significant moments between you and your leader?

_____
_____
_____
_____

Why was it important for Elisha to leave right?

_____
_____
_____
_____

Why did Elisha need to be processed after he was chosen?

_____
_____
_____
_____

Why did Elijah keep trying to leave Elisha?

_____
_____
_____
_____

Why did the other prophets try to discourage Elisha?

_____
_____
_____
_____

What does it means to receive a double portion?

_____
_____
_____
_____

How would you explain having the SPIRIT of your leader?

_____
_____
_____
_____

Why was it Important for Elisha to call him Father?

_____
_____
_____
_____

Once Elisha received the mantle, what did he do?

_____
_____
_____
_____

Is the successor supposed to start where their leader started or stopped?

_____
_____
_____
_____

5

HONORING YOUR FATHER

In this final chapter I want to talk about honoring your father. Let's look at the scriptural basis for this in Malachi 1:6 which says: "A son honoureth his father, and a servant his master: if then I be a father, where is mine honour..." This scripture literally says if a son has a father then his father should receive honor. Then it asks the question where is my honor which means that the honor has to be in a specific place. There are three things that I want to lift up that deals with where the honor should be. First, you have to honor your father though position.

The Bible says in Psalm 133;
"...How good and pleasant it is for brethren to dwell together in unity! It is like the precious ointment upon the head, that ran down upon the beard, even Aaron's beard: that went down to the skirts of his garments; As the dew of Hermon, and as the dew that descended upon the mountains of Zion: for there the LORD commanded the blessing, even life for evermore."

There are three things that I want to share from this text:
- This text reveals that the oil flows from the head down which means there must be order.
- Then the oil flows down the face which means there has to be identity.
- The oil then has to flow down his beard which means there has to be maturity.

If there is a flow from the top down then as a son you have to contribute to that flow. Which means even if the leader has more then you your job is to make sure that there is enough in the flow to make sure that you can receive. Now, this is totally different from the way average people think. Average people think I will keep what I have and then they can sow into me so that I can be better. However, the Bible tells us that whatever you want to get then that is what you are going to have to give. So if you are going to receive from the flow of your leader then you have to sow into that flow as well.

You cannot have the attitude that you are just in their lives to take. There is one quote that I read that I really like that says, "Givers have to set boundaries because takers never do." Givers have to make sure that they position themselves properly so that they don't just give and give and give and never surround themselves with people who will give back to them. So, as a son you have to sow into that flow.

Then, there has to be identity.
Let's look at Matthew 16:13-16 which says:
"When Jesus came into the coasts of Caesarea Philippi, he asked his disciples, saying, Whom do men say that I the Son of man am? And they said, Some say that thou art John the Baptist: some, Elias; and other Jeremias, or one of the prophets. He saith unto them, But whom say ye that I am? And Simon Peter answered and said, Thou art the Christ, the Son of the living God."

I want to share with you what I believe Jesus was really saying to his disciples. When He asked who do the men say that I am, what He meant was what is the censes about Me among the masses. I don't walk or talk with them. All I do is perform miracles but I spend time with all of you. I want to know what the people have to say about me but then I also want to know what all of you have to say about who I am.

The disciples were closer to the people then Jesus. I believe that this was a rebuke that Jesus gave them. I believe that He was literally saying how is it that when you see Me you see the Father but when they see you they don't see Me. What this means is if you are a son people should see an extension of the person that you are connected with. So there has to be identity there. There should be some similarities between you and your leader. If the person that you are submitted to is good enough for you to be submitted to them then they should also be good enough for you to pattern.

Then there has to be maturity. Leaders always have to test maturity. They watch what your response is when you have to get rebuked. They watch how you handle obstacles and opposition. They watch to see when you go through things if you feel like quitting all the time. They are looking to see if you are impatient or have a zero tolerance for opposition or problems. All of that will tell the leader how mature you are. If you talk more then you listen or if you talk more then you see then that tells the leader that you are not mature. If your business is shared among a whole lot of people and not just your inner circle that tells the leader that you are immature.

So, if there is going to be a flow then it has to hit all of those areas of maturity. Not your level of giftedness but your level of maturity. Maturity comes upon character and not upon talents. You can be the greatest preacher, singer, or worker but if your character is not where it should be then that flow is not going to come to you. One of the things that I have learned that is important is not only must you be able to love the father but you have to love what and who he loves. When it comes to whoever is connected to him you never want to be found killing the very thing that he wants alive. You have to make sure that if you are a son that you love what your father loves.

The Bible says that the brethren must dwell together in unity. This deals with the flow. Again the Bible says how pleasant it is for the brethren. It did not say how good and pleasant it is for the fathers and the sons to assemble. This says that even if the father is not present the sons still have to gather together to make sure that they create unity among the camp. I always say that most churches are not growing and it is not because a mature word is not being preached but because there is division, envy, and strife among those that are in the pews. So, whenever the leader sows a Filet Mignon Word if there is strife among the people in the audience by the time that Word goes across the altar it is no longer filet mignon but similac. The strife reduced the effectiveness of the power of that word and God is not going to give us meat when we only qualify for milk.

The Bible basis for that is 1 Corinthians 3:1-3 let's look at that:
"And I, brethren, could not speak unto you as unto spiritual, but as unto carnal, even as unto babes in Christ. I have fed you with milk, and not with meat: for hitherto ye were not able to bear it, neither yet now are ye able. For ye are yet carnal: for whereas there is among you envying, and strife, and divisions, are ye not carnal, and walk as men?"

Paul tells them in Corinthians that you are carnal and I know that you are carnal because there is envy, strife, and divisions among you. Jealousy is when you don't want someone to have something but envy is when you wish you had what is theirs. Division is separatism, cliques, your own individual groups within the group and that speaks again to your carnality. The Bible says where strife is there is room for every evil work. Paul was telling them flat out because you present a level of carnality I cannot give you meat.

When the sons gather together in unity to work hard, to make sure that divisions are killed, that cliques are busted up, and that scandals are reduced, that is what continues the flow from the top down. It has to flow from the head down to the rest. It has to go from the head to the face to the beard then it has to go to the skirt which is the rest of the people. We have to work hard to dwell together in unity.

First, you honor your leader through position. Secondly, you honor your leader through pattern. Jesus told His disciples if you believe on Me you will do the works that I do and then greater works shall you do. On the surface it looks to me that Jesus was saying if you want to be great then you have to do it like I do it. The revelation for this is Jesus was saying that you do not qualify for greater, until you can, do it the way that I do it. The reality is that as sons you do not qualify for greater works because you have an idea, but you qualify for greater works when you can be trusted.

Jesus said that you have to first believe in Me and if you believe in Me then you are going to do the works that I do. That exposes the fact that maybe sons are not really committed to their fathers because they don't do what they do. If you believed in them then you would do it like they do it, because you would want to get the results of their obedience and their activity. In the church that I came from, we did not have praise and worship, we had devotion. We didn't have everyone standing, lifting their hands, going into what we call worship. We had the devotion with a deacon kneeling down, whooping his prayer while he prayed and then we would sing with him after. I wanted to shift into praise and worship but I was under my biological father who was a traditional Baptist pastor. If I was ever going to qualify for greater works I had to prove to him that I could be trusted with devotion before I could ever get exposed to praise and worship.

So, as a son if you believe that God has given you a greater way of getting the job done then don't get mad because they won't let you immediately change it. Just make sure that you are able to do it the way that they do it. If they want you to preach with points, then preach with points. If they want you to stand on the floor and not in the pulpit, then stand where they want you to stand because it is more about being trusted then being talented. When you are talented you will have giftings and abilities but when you are trusted you will have opportunities to be to able to showcase that gifting and ability. Greater works is the ability to take what the leader gave you and do it at a greater level. That means if you are connected to them then you do not start over but you always build off of where they left off.

First, you honor your leader through position. Secondly, you honor them through pattern. Now, this is the final thing that is difficult for most people to understand. You have to honor your father through your possessions. As a real son one of the greatest joys I've ever had was being a blessing to my father. I have seen his heart and I have seen how hard he has worked. I have seen so many people come in and take or miss use his heart and his act of kindness. However, I have always found pleasure in being able to give and be a blessing to him. I had searched for many years for real connecting so I have been committed to honoring him.
I have seen the drastic change as a pastor in the financial status of my local church. I've seen us hit numbers while I was on my own tithing to my church. Then I have also seen our numbers grow when I began to tithe to the very thing that I was connected to.

When you deal with the biblical basis of tithing you will understand that a tithe is considered as the heave offering. That means that you never sow it to you, something that is on your level, or something that is under you. You always take the tithe and sow it to what is above you. Now, you are a part of a church which means that you are on the same level of the church. However, whoever your spiritual father is that is the person that is above you and that is where the tithe should be placed. Again, you have to sow to where you want the flow from.

I have not yet understood how pastors can submit to someone but never give to that very thing. You have to put your money where your mouth is. In Matthew 6:21 the Bible says "where your treasure is there will your heart be also." In Matthew 12:34 the Bible says "out of the abundance of the heart the mouth speaks." This means that whatever you love your money is going to be there. Then wherever your heart is that is where your mouth is.

What we end up doing is we use our mouth to say that we love but never use our money to back up the fact that our heart is in the right place and that we are not just giving words.

It is easy on a holiday or on a pastor's anniversary to say as a son that I love my father and give to him. However, the real test is where have you placed your possessions and have you been a blessing to them. When you bless them it does not always have to be seen by others. Sometimes you have to do it in secret and the Bible says whatever you do in secret the Father will reward you openly. So, again if you are submitted to them then you want to sow to them. You want to make sure that they are ok. You want to make sure that they understand that you are not just giving lip service alone because again where your treasure is there will your heart be also.

Matthew 6:21, 12:34 these scriptures reveal that your money should be where your mouth is. Giving is not only a part of worship but giving is worship. The more you give then the more blessed you will be because your obedience is your greatest honor. The sacrifice and the dollar amount is great but what is greater is your obedience. You have to know the fact that you are submitted and that you always have to play a valuable role in the life of your leader. Giving is not about the amount but giving is about sacrifice. If I have $5.00 and I give $3.00 then that is a greater sacrifice then someone that has $1,000,000 and gives $100,000. God is going to reward you based upon your level of sacrifice.

1 Samuel 15:22 says *"And Samuel said, Hath the LORD as great delight in burnt offering and sacrifices, as in obeying the voice of the LORD? Behold, to obey is better than sacrifice, and to hearken than the fat of rams."*

So, again if you are going to honor your father then first you have to honor them in position. You have to be in place. They should never have to wonder where you are. They should never have to wonder if you are going to fulfill your assignment. As your leader is in transition they should never have to wonder if you are going to be synchronized to their moment or not. That is how you honor them through position. Secondly, you have to honor them through pattern. You have to show them that you can be trusted. You do certain things to look like them or imitate them or to walk as they walk. You find yourself saying certain things that you hear them saying on a weekly basis. Thirdly, you should honor them with your possessions.

I pray that you will receive this teaching and do something in the life of your leader to show them that not only are you close to them but you are connected to them. Also, that you know that because you are connected to them you know that you are to give to them. God will place on your heart what to give them, when to give it to them, and how to give it. I promise that will minister to your father in such a very special way.

Most times as fathers we are so used to giving far more than we are use to getting. When someone decides to break the mold and give unto us and not just take, that qualifies them to be trusted for private moments and private opportunities. You never know what that is going to unlock in your own personal life, because what you make happen for someone else God will make happen for you. Do not dare to make it happen for someone who is not responsible for your soul. As the watchman of your soul your possessions should always be with your leader. So that they always know that if they cannot count on anyone, that they can always count on their sons.

You have to ask yourself if you are that son that can be counted on. Ask yourself, are you in position, in place, on time, and do you represent them right. Ask yourself if you are a good pattern of your leader. Are you reflecting the standards, the beliefs, and the convictions of that leader? Then ask yourself if you are making sure that you are honoring your father with your possessions. If you are doing all of that, then you are qualifying for the next step in sonship.

CONVERSATION STARTERS

What does the word HONOR mean to you?

_____
_____
_____
_____

What does honor mean to your leader?

_____
_____
_____
_____

Do you believe that the anointing flows from the top down? If so or if not, explain.

_____
_____
_____
_____

How do you help to contribute to that flow?

_____
_____
_____
_____

Is your leader worth imitating?

_____
_____
_____
_____

What adjustments have you made spiritually or naturally because of your leader's example?

_____

_____

_____

_____

What has been the hardest adjustment you've made because of your leader's example?

_____

_____

_____

_____

Do you believe your leader trusts you? Rate from 1-10.

_____

_____

_____

_____

What can you do to increase the level of trust between you and your leader?

_____

_____

_____

_____

How often do you sow into the life of your leader?

_____

_____

_____

_____

What are the ways you sow into the life of your leader?

_____

_____

_____

_____

If money was not an option, what would you do to help your leader's vision come to pass?

_____

_____

_____

_____

6

FINAL WORDS

It has been my desire to convey what I believe to be the mind of God as it relates to this matter of sonship. Malachi 4:6 declares "And he shall turn the heart of the fathers to the children, and the heart of the children to their fathers, lest I come and smite the earth with a curse." It is my prayer that this book will serve as a guide for those seeking clarity and instruction to be a better servant and a better son. We all know that the need for titles and position has become a contagious disease around the world. However, what I have discovered is that the mantle always falls or flows to the son and not just those that are serving.

I do not want you to miss what the Father has in store for you. You don't have to start anything out of anger, disappointment, or out of frustration. You can walk in succession as it relates to faithfulness because I have handled this understanding positively and negatively. I beseech you to take in these written words as God's instructions to you. You want to make sure that you are qualified to be a son and not a bastard. Not someone that is so headstrong and believes that they can make decisions for themselves. You have to be someone that is trusted into this process called sonship.

These chapters were uniquely articulated to serve as not just a reading but also as a manual to help you execute these principles starting today. Those that you are submitted to should see a visible difference in your life because you have read this. You will be able to sustain this difference as this begins to be a daily manual for you and those that are connected to you. The hearts of the real fathers are very sensitive and valuable. Many have hurt the same heart that has been given the assignment to love you. As a result of these hurts your assignment is also to bring healing to those that you are connected to. Also, as you help to heal them they will help to heal you.

The joy in this is that both parties will grow together and appreciate the process after the healing has taken place. In the next volume of this important subject of sonship, I will discuss some equally essential issues from the father's perspective. I dare not challenge you to be submitted to a concept or a person that is not submitted to their purpose to you as well. I dare not lead you into bondage and allow abuse to be executed through the mask of sonship and authority. You will learn the role of the father. You will also learn how to help the father as a submitted son who chooses to honor him not just as a yes man but as a man who has been called to serve. If I write the next book will you read it?

ABOUT THE AUTHOR

Johnasen L. Pack: Born prematurely in Texarkana, Texas, it was clear that the world was given a gift ahead of schedule. Pastor Pack received his call to preach at nine years old. He rejected that call and began participating in gang activity and violence for the next six years. God allowed and used these experiences to prepare him for a relevant ministry. He was saved at the age of fifteen, was licensed to preach at seventeen, and was ordained at nineteen.

Pastor Pack served as Youth Pastor, assisted the music and prison ministries, and served his father, Pastor Johnny Pack IV, faithfully at the Fellowship Missionary Baptist Church. In March of 2001, Pastor Pack organized the New Generation Revival Church in Portland, Oregon. In 2003, he became one of the youngest Overseers in the Full Gospel Baptist Church Fellowship, serving 6 churches in the Portland area. In 2007 Pastor Pack moved families from the New Generation Revival Church of Portland, Oregon to Arlington, Texas and organized the Bridge Builders International Church where he currently pastors.

With over a decade of ministry, Pastor Pack has traveled the country preaching and presenting an empowering message of healing and deliverance to all ages. Known for his revelation of "SONSHIP," he has become an influential voice of his generation. Pastor Pack has made numerous appearances on TBN as both a speaker and a host. He is also a life coach, author motivational speaker, spiritual father, and with all of his accomplishments, he celebrates his brilliant and beautiful children.

With his unique style of preaching and teaching, every hearer will receive the tools to face and conquer life's day to day challenges. Pastor Pack is a visionary. He is not just a leader in the fundamental sense; he is becoming an influential voice for a new generation of people who are seeking answers amidst the confusion of religious philosophy, and propels audiences to a sincere and enjoyable relationship with Jesus Christ.

For more information about Johnasen L. Pack visit:
www.JLPMnow.org